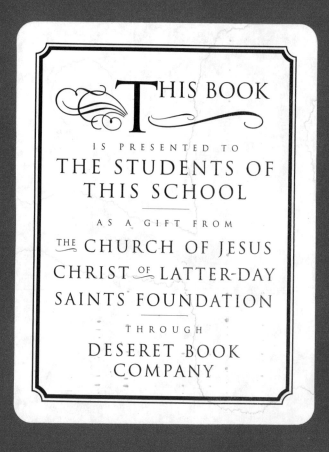

The Gargoyle on the Roof

POEMS BY

JACK PRELUTSKY

PICTURES BY

PETER SÍS

GREENWILLOW BOOKS, NEW YORK

The full-color art was reproduced from
oil and gouache paintings on a gesso background.
The text type is Della Robbia Bold.

Library of Congress Cataloging-in-Publication Data

Prelutsky, Jack.
The gargoyle on the roof /
by Jack Prelutsky : illustrations by Peter Sís.
p.   cm.
Summary: Presents poems about gargoyles, vampires,
the bogeyman, gremlins, and other monsters.
ISBN 0-688-09643-3 (trade).   ISBN 0-688-16553-2 (lib. bdg.)
1. Children's poetry, American.   2. Fantasy poetry, American.
[1. Monsters—Poetry.   2. American poetry.]   I. Sís, Peter, ill.
II. Title   PS3566.R36G37   1999
811'.54—dc21   99-10578   CIP

FOR JUDSON AND SIMEON

—J. P.

FOR ADRIAN LASZLO BLOOMER

—P. S.

CONTENTS

I'M NOT OPEN FOR AN HOUR

I'm not open for an hour,
But there's much that I must do,
Like concocting extra gallons
Of conditioning shampoo.
There are lotions to be blended,
Gels and mousses to prepare,
For my clients are afflicted
With unmanageable hair.

All my bobby pins are ready,
My barrettes are in a line,
I've assembled combs and brushes
Fit to groom a porcupine.
I have honed a hundred razors
Made with heavy-duty blades,
Chosen ribbons for my patrons
Who wear ponytails or braids.

I am sorting through my curlers,
I am sharpening my shears,
Rearranging special clippers
Best for trimming tails and ears.
I have hired six assistants
Who don't mind an angry bite—
I'm the werewolves' master barber,
And the moon is full tonight.

6

LAMENT OF A LONELY TROLL

I am, alas, a lonely troll,
My days are all the same,
I seldom see a single soul,
My neighbors fear my name.
Because I'm gruesome, grim, and gruff,
I've had no guests for years.
The situation's bad enough
To drive a troll to tears.

I'm destined, it appears to me,
To live my life alone,
But, desperate for company,
I've bought a telephone.
Feel free to call me, night or day,
No matter if I slumber,
And furthermore, you need not pay—
I've got a troll-free number.

8

9

10

MOTHER GARGOYLE'S LULLABY

The moon and stars have vanished,
The long dark night is through,
Another day is dawning,
The sky is clear and blue.
The morning sun is rising,
It's climbing overhead.
My precious baby gargoyles
Should snuggle into bed.

It's time to sheathe your talons
And fold your stony wings,
For when you sweetly slumber,
You do not need these things.
Dream your lovely daymares,
Where terror is delight,
And when the moon and stars return,
We'll soar throughout the night.

PLAINT OF THE HEADLESS HORSEMAN

Beside my steed I sadly stand,
My severed head in my right hand,
Sorrowed that you sped away—
I simply asked the time of day.

13

BUGABOO

I'm Bugaboo the bogeyman,
Perhaps you've heard of me.
I'm meaner than a bogeyman
Has any need to be.
I've earned my reputation
By my manner and my style.
I'm truly reprehensible,
Malodorous and vile.

My eyes are red, my hair is green,
I wear a frightful scowl.
My features are ferocious,
And my breath is always foul.
I strive to be unsavory
In every way I can—
At times I've even terrified
The other bogeyman.

You'd better never misbehave
When Bugaboo's about.
I'm apt to snatch you by your ears
And turn you inside out.
Don't disregard this warning
If you know what's good for you.
I am the dreaded bogeyman,
My name is Bugaboo!

15

A VAMPIRE SPEAKS OF GROOMING

When I look into the mirror,
My reflection's never there.
So I always stare at nothing
As I shave and comb my hair.

I AM RUNNING THROUGH A TUNNEL

I am running through a tunnel
Where there isn't any sun.
There's an ogre right behind me,
Running faster than I run.
It is gaining every second,
Though I'm going very fast.
I'm undoubtedly in trouble
When it catches me at last.

It's reputed that the creature
Has the strength of twenty men.
Should I happen to elude it,
I'll not visit here again.
But the beast has almost caught me,
Though I practically fly.
Now I feel its breath upon me—
Now I'm in its grasp . . . good-bye!

SONG OF THE BABY GARGOYLES

We love you, Mother Gargoyle dear,
We positively do.
No other baby gargoyles
Have a mother sweet as you.
And Mother, since we know how much
you love the three of us,
We're sure you'll grant our little wish
Without your normal fuss.

We do not want to go to bed,
We want to stay awake,
And see what sort of merriment
And mischief we can make.
We're not the least bit drowsy,
Really, truly, not at all,
It's such a waste of time to sleep
All day atop a wall.

We want to stay awake and play,
To rise into the sky.
The thought of going straight to bed
Just makes us want to cry.
We want to soar above the streets
And plummet through the air,
To terrify pedestrians—
They're so much fun to scare.

And if you let us stay awake
Till noon, or even ten,
We promise we will never ask
For anything again.
We'll be three perfect demons
Every minute of the year—
So do not make us go to bed,
Please, Mother Gargoyle dear.

MY SISTER IS A WEREWOLF

My sister is a werewolf,
It's disquieting and strange.
One moonlit night I watched her
Undergo a sudden change.
Her arms and face grew hairy,
And her voice became a roar.
In some ways she looked better
Than she'd ever looked before.

I ran and told our parents,
Who began to fret and fuss
In despair and disapproval,
Moaning, "No! She's not like us!"
I adore my sister dearly
But reluctantly agree—
How I wish she were a vampire
Like her loving family.

BASILISK BRAG

Behold the knights aligned in fright . . .
All were noble, none were bright.
Each, upon a foolish dare,
Braved my lethal breath and stare.

My breath so sharp, my stare so hot
Petrified them on the spot.
Here those hapless knights remain,
Slowly rusting in the rain.

GOBBLEUP

I'm Gobbleup the goblin,
Unimaginably mean.
My gobliny complexion
Is a nauseating green.
My ears are long and pointy,
And my nose is pointy too,
My fangs are always ready
To make mincemeat out of you.

I'm Gobbleup the goblin,
With malicious, tiny eyes.
I love to lurk in shadows
And to catch you by surprise.
I'll pursue you through the forest
As you flee in utter fright.
The more intense your terror,
Then the deeper my delight.

My laugh is disconcerting,
And my voice is shrill and thin,
And when I pounce upon your bones,
You'll jump out of your skin.
I'm heinous, harsh, and horrible,
I have a wretched smell.
I'm Gobbleup the goblin,
And I do not wish you well.

27

BENEATH A BRIDGE

Beneath a bridge, a greedy troll
Perennially waits,
And watches with deceitful eyes
The size of dinner plates.
His face is unforgiving,
It has rarely worn a smile.
His mind is coarse and cunning,
And his heart is filled with bile.

If you would cross unhindered,
You must tender him his toll,
For only gold will satisfy
This avaricious troll.
If witlessly you undertake
To pass but not to pay,
He'll soon revoke your license
To return another day.

The troll will squeeze you mightily,
No matter how you plead,
For his anger's even stronger
Than his overwhelming greed.
If you've no wish to meet this fate,
Regard my sage advice . . .
Be cordial as you cross the bridge,
And pay the troll his price.

GUFFIN AND GIFFIN

We're Guffin and Giffin,
Unthinkable griffins.
Our wings are our fortune,
We're lords of the air.
We soar over mountains,
Descend into valleys,
Performing maneuvers
No eagles would dare.

Our faces are fearsome,
Our bodies gigantic,
Our shimmering talons
Are harder than steel.
We swoop over housetops
In search of a morsel,
A succulent human,
Our favorite meal.

We'll carry you off
If we happen to spy you.
You cannot escape
When we loom overhead.
We're Guffin and Giffin,
Unthinkable griffins . . .
If you hear us shrieking,
Hide under your bed.

A VAMPIRE SPEAKS OF CIRCUSES

I often go to circuses
To see the ponies prance.
I love the HUMAN CANNONBALL
And clowns in baggy pants.

The elephants amuse me,
I adore the DANCING RATS,
But I applaud my loudest
For the daring ACRO-BATS.

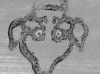

GREMLINS

When your pillow turns to pickles,
And there's honey on your head,
When you note an orange elephant
Reclining on your bed,
When you reach into your pocket
And withdraw a purple mouse,
These are early indications
There are gremlins in your house.

When your breakfast sings a solo,
And your supper tastes like soap,
When you find a dozen meatballs
Stuffed inside a cantaloupe,
When spaghetti fills the bathtub,
And the shower starts to sneeze,
You have gremlins running rampant,
Doing anything they please.

Your existence turns to chaos
When you've got a gremlin blight,
For although they're not ferocious
And are disinclined to bite,
They may make your nose fluorescent,
Cause your underwear to fall . . .
The unnatural is normal
When the gremlins come to call.

A WEREWOLF
OF DISTINCTION

I, a werewolf of distinction,
Used to fill the night with fear,
But I'm entering the twilight
Of my infamous career.
I do not engender terror,
I do not command respect,
Both my shoulders droop so badly,
I can scarcely stand erect.

When I stalked the moonlit city,
Many panicked at my cough.
Now my roar is but a whisper,
People laugh at me and scoff.
My endurance has diminished,
I am clumsy, I am slow,
And my muscles do not ripple
As they rippled long ago.

In my heart I'm still ferocious,
But my strength is growing weak,
And I'm hardly prepossessing,
For I'm losing my physique.
I could use a set of dentures,
And my fur is falling out.
If the tendency continues,
I'll be hairless as a trout.

My appetite is dwindling,
And my arms are getting thin.
My legs have turned to spindles,
And my chest is caving in.
I'm no longer fit for prowling,
I'm disheartened and appalled—
There are few who fear a werewolf
Who is toothless, frail, and bald.

THE GARGOYLE ON THE ROOF

I am the gargoyle on the roof,
My eyes are fiery red,
My claws are keen and deadly,
And my flinty wings are spread.
I perch atop my domicile
To guard it night and day.
My ears can hear your footfalls
From a thousand miles away.

I am the gargoyle on the roof,
A creature hewn of stone.
My long and lonely vigil
Is the only life I've known.
No sight escapes my tireless gaze,
My nostrils test the air.
If you have cause to enter here,
Take caution, and take care.

Those knaves whose base intention
Is to cause my house distress,
Shall know my wrathful virulence
And feel my cold caress.
I'll strike them and devour them
As an owl devours a mouse . . .
I am the gargoyle on the roof,
And I defend my house.

JACK PRELUTSKY is a household
name to poetry readers and lovers
all over the country. He has written
more than thirty books of verse, edited
several hugely popular anthologies,
and appeared in more schools and
libraries than he can count. Among
his most popular books are *The New
Kid on the Block*, *The Dragons Are
Singing Tonight*, and *Something Big
Has Been Here*. He and his wife live
in the Seattle area.

PETER SÍS received Caldecott
Honors for *Starry Messenger*, his story
of Galileo, and for *Tibet: Through the
Red Box*. He is the author-artist of many
other highly praised books, including
Fire Truck, *Trucks Trucks Trucks*, *Ship
Ahoy!*, and *Komodo!* He has illustrated
several books by Jack Prelutsky,
Sid Fleischman, and George Shannon.
He and his family live in New York City.